CITIES OF THE
WORLD

MEXICO CITY

BY R. CONRAD STEIN

CHILDREN'S PRESS®
A Division of Grolier Publishing
New York London Hong Kong Sydney
Danbury, Connecticut

CONSULTANTS

George I. Blanksten, Ph.D.
Professor Emeritus of Political Science
Northwestern University, Evanston, Illinois

Robert Somerlott, M.A.
Academic Director, Instituto Allende
San Miguel de Allende, Mexico

Project Editor: Downing Publishing Services
Design Director: Karen Kohn & Associates, Ltd.
Photo Researcher: Jan Izzo

LIBRARY OF CONGRESS CATALOGING-IN-PUBLICATION DATA

Stein, R. Conrad
 Mexico City / by R. Conrad Stein
  p. cm. — (Cities of the World)
 Includes index.
 Summary: Provides a physical description of the city as well as an overview of
  the history and customs of the capital of Mexico.
 ISBN 0-516-00352-6
 1. Mexico City (Mexico) — Juvenile literature. [1. Mexico City (Mexico)]
I. Title. II. Series: Cities of the world (New York, N.Y.)
F1386.S82 1996
972' .53 — dc20   95-36152
                                                              CIP
                                                              AC

TABLE OF CONTENTS

In the summer of 1991, much of Mexico was treated to one of nature's most stunning spectacles—a total eclipse of the sun. In Mexico City, thousands of people crowded into the large central plaza called the Zócalo. They were there to witness this once-in-a-life-time event. The throng gasped as the moon blotted out the sun, the temperature dropped twenty degrees, and stars appeared in the noonday heavens. When the awesome sky show ended, a newspaper reporter asked people why they chose to view it from the Zócalo. "Because," said many spectators, "the Zócalo is a magical place."

The Zócalo

Everyone calls Mexico City's great central square the Zócalo, but its official name is the *Plaza de la Constitución* (Constitution Plaza). The word *zócalo* means base or foundation. Shortly after Mexico won its independence from Spain in 1821, government leaders decided to build a statue in the plaza. It was to be dedicated to their newfound freedom. But the leaders could not agree on what kind of statue they should erect. As a result, only the base was built. For decades during the 1800s, the unadorned base (or zócalo) stood in the square. Mexico City residents began calling the entire grounds the Zócalo, and the name stuck—even after the empty pedestal was removed. Today, the central plazas of many Mexican towns are called zócalos after the main square in Mexico City.

Plaza de la Constitución (PLAH-SAH DEH LAH KON-STEE-TOO-SEE-OHN)
Zócalo (SOH-KAH-LOH)

There has always been magic in the Zócalo. Almost seven hundred years ago, the Aztecs claimed that a powerful god commanded them to build a city. What is now the Zócalo was to be its center. Over the centuries, the plaza has witnessed the dramatic events that shaped Mexican history: the fall of the Aztecs, the rise of the Spanish Empire, the

The man shown below knows that he will find customers for his baskets at the Zócalo (above).

Mexican War of Independence, and a bloody civil war. No other spot on earth is more sacred to Mexicans than this square. People get married in the plaza (above), they sing there, and they cry tears of joy there. It is the soul of a nation and the heart of a great city. There is no better place to begin the Mexico City story than at the Zócalo.

STREETS

Mexico City is the capital of Mexico. Each year, thousands of travelers from foreign lands visit the city. Most visitors flock to the glass and steel hotels that rise along the city's famous boulevards—Insurgentes and the Reforma. But just a few blocks from the beautiful boulevards spread humble neighborhoods where tourists rarely venture. Those neighborhoods support an exciting street life. The Mexico City streets are a playground, a theater, a marketplace, and a special world pulsating with life.

A LOOK AT THE STREET VENDORS

Want to buy a pair of shoelaces? Look around. You are sure to find a shoelace seller standing on the sidewalk. A tray is anchored to his belt and held in place by a strap around his neck. The tray contains shoelaces of all sizes and colors. Want to buy a candy bar? Again, look around. You'll soon see a man or a woman sitting in front of a plastic tarp upon which is a great array of candy bars. Walk the streets long enough and you'll find vendors selling pots and pans, live chickens and turkeys, power tools, TVs, VCRs, and even computers.

No one knows how many street vendors operate in Mexico City. There may be millions. Many, many people must sell goods in the streets just to survive. Jobs are scarce, and the minimum wage is only sixteen pesos a day. Sixteen pesos is barely enough to buy a large hamburger, fries, and a malt at one of the capital's many McDonald's restaurants. A hard-working street vendor can earn twice or three times the minimum wage.

This woman is selling homemade hats for children to wear on January 6. That day is La Epifanía, the Feast of the Three Kings.

Not all Mexico City vendors operate on the streets of the city. This young man is helping his family at their floating restaurant on a Xochimilco canal.

Xochimilco
(SOH-SHEE-MEEL-KOH)

Because they number so many, the street vendors must work very hard to make a living. An elderly woman selling lottery tickets rushes up to people shouting, "Do you want to be a millionaire today? Of course you do. Buy my tickets. They'll make you rich."

A thin young man roams the traffic-clogged streets waving a fistful of windshield-wiper blades above his head. A driver nods to him, and with flying fingers the young man changes wiper blades on the car while the driver waits at a red light.

Owners of stores complain that street sellers pay no rent or taxes, and therefore have an unfair advantage over them. City authorities say the sellers' stands make the sidewalks overcrowded. But the Mexico City public accepts and even applauds the street merchants. Buying from them is convenient, and their goods are often cheaper than those available at the stores. The vendors also act as a silent police force of the sidewalks. Violent crime is rare in the city. Feathery-fingered pickpockets do work their mischief in the crowds, but only on occasion is someone robbed at gunpoint. The vendors form an army of potential witnesses who see everything around them. Residents believe they discourage violent criminals.

The young girl shown above sells flowers on the streets of Mexico City. Other street vendors sell such things as shoelaces, candy bars, and windshield-wiper blades.

The most numerous of all the street vendors are those who sell prepared food. Mexico City dwellers prefer to eat their main meal—*la comida*—at midday. At night, they have snacks. They buy the snacks at thousands of stands that sell cut-up fruit, ice cream, pastries, *tortas* (sandwiches made from crusty rolls), and, of course, tacos. At taco stands, fried meat, stews, or cheese concoctions are rolled into tortillas. They are dished out to customers who usually eat standing up. The smell of tacos sizzling in oil is a symbol of Mexico City street life.

Children buy candy skulls from vendors on a feast day called the Day of the Dead.

la comida (LA KOH-MEE-DAH)

12

Many Mexico City dwellers buy their evening meals at taco stands like this one.

A Delightful Climate

"Warm and sunny." These words describe nearly any day of the year in Mexico City. During the day, one rarely needs a jacket, even in the "cold" months from December through February. Also, it almost never feels too hot. That's because the capital is in a valley about 7,500 feet above sea level. It is cooled by mountain air. The only exception to the warm and sunny conditions comes from June through September. That's the rainy season, when the city gets drenching rains and sometimes violent storms. Mexico City's delightful weather encourages an out-of-doors lifestyle and fosters its fascinating world of the streets.

THE STREET ENTERTAINERS

He calls himself *Jorge el Gordo*—Fat George. When asked his weight, he laughs and says, "Oh, maybe 120 kilos [roughly 270 pounds] more or less." More is the better guess. Fat George stands on a downtown street corner wearing a yellow clown suit. He blows up long balloons and twists them together to create figures of dogs, donkeys, spiders, and giraffes. When a family with a small child passes by, Fat George makes a funny face and holds up one of his balloon sculptures. The child pesters the parents to buy one, they agree, and Fat George makes a peso or two. "I live on laughter," he says.

Fat George is a street entertainer. He is one of many who try to capture people's interest in return for a few coins. The entertainers include clowns, jugglers, tumblers, mimes, and magicians. Children as young as ten years old board city buses where they play the harmonica and sing. When their "act" is over, they pass a hat among the passengers. The showmen and women make up a cast of thousands who perform daily and produce an amazing theater-on-the-street in the Mexican capital.

The people who entertain on the streets of Mexico City include clowns, jugglers, tumblers, magicians, balloon sellers—and even organ grinders like this one.

The most spectacular—and the craziest—
of the street entertainers are the *tragafuegos,* the
fire-eaters. Mostly teenaged boys, they appear on the
sidewalks at dusk carrying a can of gasoline and a lighted
torch. When a crowd gathers, the *tragafuego* takes a
mouthful of gasoline, holds the torch in front of his lips, and
blows out. A finger of flame ten or twelve feet long shoots out
of his mouth. Spectators ooh and aah at the sight. But many onlookers
shake their heads sadly. They know these boys are burning their lungs to ashes in
their effort to make a living in Mexico City.

*The fire-eaters of Mexico City
are called* tragafuegos. *They
always draw excited crowds, but
eating fire is a very dangerous
way to try to make a living.*

All city dwellers enjoy *mariachis,* the world-famous strolling musicians. A *mariachi* band is made up of six to eight men with horns, violins, and guitars. They wear tight-fitting black costumes and broad cartwheel hats. Their favorite gathering place is Plaza Garibaldi in the heart of downtown. On a good night, as many as twenty bands crowd into the plaza. They pump out twenty different songs all at the same time. Throngs of laughing people follow the wild beats in Plaza Garibaldi. It is the centerpiece of the city's joyous street entertainment scene.

This mariachi *trumpet player is wearing
the traditional black costume with a broad
cartwheel hat.*

THE STREETS AS A PLAYGROUND

Naranja dulce,
NAH-RAHN-HAH DOOL-SEH

Limon partido
LEE-MONE PAHR-TEE-DOH

Dame un abrazo
DAH-MEH OON AH-BRAH-SOH

Que yo te pido,
KEH YOH TEH PEE-DOH

Sweet Orange,

Sliced Lemon

Give me a hug

That I ask for.

These children are playing the circle game called Naranja Dulce.

These words are sung during the street game *Naranja Dulce*. It is played by small children in Mexico City. While singing, the children hold hands and twirl in a circle. When the song gets to the "give me a hug" part, everyone stops and hugs and kisses the closest person. Maybe a child doesn't particularly like that person, but kisses have to be given—rules of the game.

Most children in Mexico City are poor and have few toys. Also, playgrounds with swings and slides are scarce. So the sidewalks become playgrounds, and children create their own games. Most of the games are played to the tune of songs that have snappy rhymes. One jump-rope chant gives a quick recipe for the famous Mexican stew *pozole:* "*Carne, chili, mole . . . pozole.*" Translated the words mean, "Meat, chili peppers, sauce [makes] pozole stew."

Carne, chili, mole . . . pozole (KAHR-NEH, CHEE-LEH, MOH-LEH . . . POH-SOH-LEH)

el avian (EL AH-VEE-AHN)

El Avian

The Mexico City version of hopscotch is a sidewalk game called *el avian* (the flyer). Using chalk, a player draws squares on the sidewalk numbered 1 through 9. A large circle, labeled 10, marks the end of the contest. To begin, one or more children take a couple of sheets of wet newspaper and wad them up until they become very messy balls. The players then throw the newspaper balls onto a numbered square. Another player, hopping on one foot, advances square by square, but must jump over the square in which a wet paper ball lies. The child who reaches number 10 first wins—if he doesn't first fall flat on his face.

By United States standards, Mexico City is ancient. It is the oldest continuously occupied city on the American continent. So old is this city that its beginnings are mingled with legend.

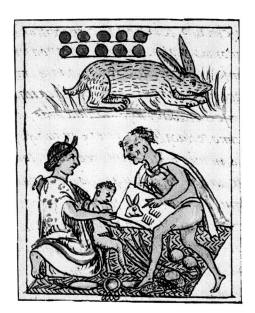

The ancient Aztecs of Mexico City used picture writing (pictography) like this to make books. The page on the left shows Aztec soldiers conquering cities as they built their powerful empire. The picture above shows Aztec parents teaching their child about his lucky day.

THE PROMISE OF A GOD

According to legend, the Aztec people once lived in a lovely, well-watered land called Aztlan. For unknown reasons, the small group of Aztecs abandoned Aztlan. They began searching for a new home in the deserts of northern Mexico. Their most treasured possession was a statue of a god called Huitzilopochtli, the hummingbird. Priests claimed they were able to speak with the god through the statue. The god told them to look for a place where they would see an eagle perched on a cactus while eating a snake. On that spot they were to build a city.

Huitzilopochtli (above) was the Aztec god whose name means "The Hummingbird."

Tradition says the Aztecs wandered for one hundred years before they entered the green and fertile Valley of Mexico. It was a forested region dotted by lakes. Over the centuries, great civilizations had risen in the valley. The Aztecs—the nomads of the north—looked in awe at magnificent stone cities. Still homeless, the Aztec people became mercenary soldiers. They fought battles for the settled people.

Huitzilopochtli (WHEET-SEE-LOH-POH-SHLEE)
Tenochtitlán (TEH-NO-SHTEET-LAN)

An eagle perched on a cactus while eating a snake appears on the back of Mexico's one-peso and two-peso coins.

This illustration shows the origins of the founding of the great Aztec city Tenochtitlán. According to legend, the god Huitzilopochtli told the Aztecs to build a city on the spot where they saw an eagle perched on a cactus.

This picture shows the temple district in the center of Tenochtitlán, the great Aztec capital.

Finally, at the southern end of the valley, the Aztecs saw the promise of their god: an eagle perched on a cactus while eating a snake. This miracle occurred on a muddy island in the middle of the broad but shallow Lake Texcoco. According to Aztec historians, the sighting took place in the year 1325. Immediately, the Aztecs began building a city. It grew to become the capital of a powerful nation. It was one of the most wondrous cities ever built. The Aztecs called their capital Tenochtitlán, Place of the Cactus.

An old illustration of an Aztec priest

FORGING AN EMPIRE

Once they were settled, the superb Aztec soldiers began forging an empire. They first conquered neighboring cities in the Valley of Mexico. Then they spread their might in every direction. At the height of its power in the early 1500s, the Aztec Empire ranged from the Atlantic Ocean to the Pacific Ocean and from the deserts of northern Mexico to the rain forests of the south. Five million to six million people lived under Aztec rule.

The hub of this great empire was the Aztec capital of Tenochtitlán. It was an island city surrounded on all sides by the sparkling waters of Lake Texcoco. Canals crisscrossed the heart of the city. They allowed boats to bring in goods for the markets. Into the city flowed the wealth of empire. Its marketplace was a magical square. Vendors sold fruit and flowers, rubber and honey, fine gold jewelry, feather blankets blazing with color, and live jaguars taken from the southern jungles. Homes of rich families were plastered with lime. They gleamed like silver in the sun. The Aztec emperor lived in a palace that had one hundred rooms, three courtyards, and a zoo.

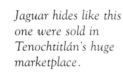

Jaguar hides like this one were sold in Tenochtitlán's huge marketplace.

This page from an Aztec book of picture writing describes certain events in the daily life of the people.

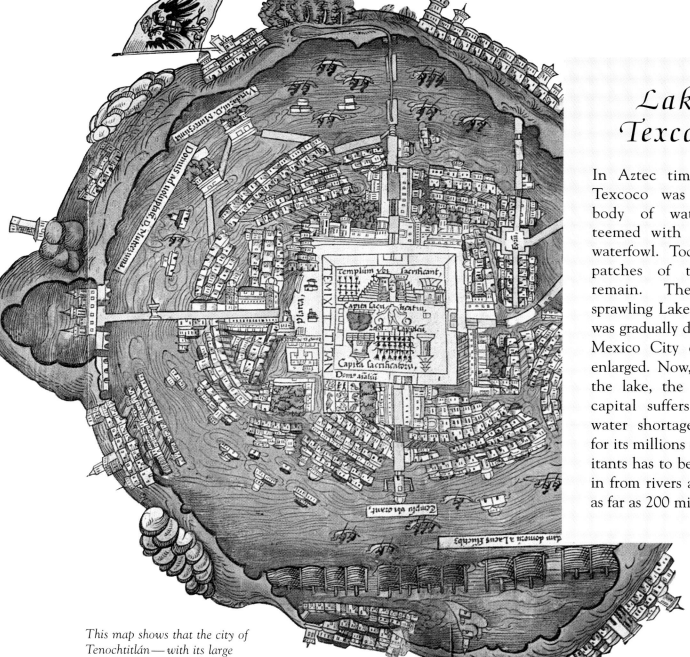

Lake Texcoco

In Aztec times, Lake Texcoco was a large body of water that teemed with fish and waterfowl. Today, only patches of the lake remain. The once-sprawling Lake Texcoco was gradually drained so Mexico City could be enlarged. Now, without the lake, the Mexican capital suffers from a water shortage. Water for its millions of inhabitants has to be pumped in from rivers and lakes as far as 200 miles away.

This map shows that the city of Tenochtitlán — with its large central marketplace, straight streets, and many canals — was surrounded by the sparkling waters of Lake Texcoco.

Texcoco (TEHS-KOH-KOH)

23

THE CITY AND THE GODS

Pyramids topped with temples stood in the center of the city. They were built in honor of the gods. The tallest of the pyramids stood as high as a modern eight-story building. It was dedicated to the hummingbird god. Here Aztec priests went about the grisly work of human sacrifice. Long lines of sacrificial victims were led up the pyramid steps. Most of them were prisoners of war. One by one, they were held over a sacrificial stone. A priest cut open the victim's chest with a razor-sharp knife. Another priest reached inside and pulled out the heart to present to the statue of a god. To Aztec thinking, the bloody gift made the god strong and helped him fight evil. The hungriest god was Huitzilopochtli, the hummingbird, who was the sun god and war god. If the hummingbird did not receive human hearts, he would not be able to rise in the morning and battle the evils of darkness.

Aztec priests sacrificing a human being to the powerful god Huitzilopochtli

Templo Mayor (TEM-PLOH MYE-OHR)

Templo Mayor (*Main Temple*), *an Aztec pyramid complex that was uncovered near the Zócalo, is now preserved as an outdoor museum.*

The priest shown in this old Mexican manuscript is holding a string of human hearts that will be sacrificed to one of the Aztec gods.

Coatlicue (KWAHT-LEE-KOO-EH)

This is Coatlicue, the Mother of the Gods.

The Aztecs believed that human sacrifice also brought victory to their army and added to the richness of their city. At its peak, Tenochtitlán spread over five square miles and held 60,000 buildings. In the early 1500s, nearly 300,000 people lived there. It may have been the largest city in the world. Its canals, its ruler-straight streets, and its towering pyramids filled visitors with wonder. An Aztec poet wrote:

The city is spread out in circles of jade.
Radiating flashes of light . . .
Beside it the lords are borne in boats;
Over them extends a flowering mist.

It seemed that the great city and the Aztec nation would last forever. But both would be destroyed by a determined band of foreigners. In 1519, some 600 Spanish soldiers landed on Mexican shores. Their commander, Hernán Cortés, asked the coastal people where he would find gold. The coastal people pointed inland and said, "Mexico." It was the word they used for the Aztec capital of Tenochtitlán. The Spaniards marched, and after a long trek they approached the outskirts of a city. It rose like a shining jewel in the green valley.

Aztec ruler Montezuma welcomed Spaniard Hernán Cortés to Tenochtitlán.

A view of Tenochtitlán showing the pyramids built in honor of the gods

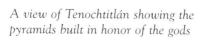

guzmā.   michuacā.

Cortés and his soldiers (below) went to war against the Aztecs (left) and eventually defeated them.

"We were amazed," wrote one Spaniard, "and said it was like the enchantments they tell of in legends. . . . Some of our soldiers asked whether the things that we saw were not a dream."

A terrible war soon broke out between Spaniards and Aztecs. In 1521, Cortés and the Spaniards defeated the Aztec nation. During the fighting, Tenochtitlán was reduced to a smoldering ruin. Never again would the magnificent Aztec city dazzle visitors with its size, beauty, and grandeur.

GHOSTS OF TENOCHTITLÁN

After the conquest, Cortés began the huge job of building a new city over the ashes of the old. He renamed it Mexico City. Though Mexico City was built in a Spanish style, Cortés kept much of the city plan the Aztecs had used for Tenochtitlán. The area that is now the Zócalo was a public gathering place in Aztec times. The site was also used as a public square under the Spaniards. Spanish engineers wrecked the huge pyramid of the hummingbird. They built a Catholic church in its place. That church is now the National Cathedral. It stands on the north side of the Zócalo. Many of the houses constructed by the Spaniards used building blocks taken from dismantled pyramids. Even today, a few of Mexico City's oldest buildings have walls made of stones that once belonged to Aztec structures.

For three hundred years, Mexico remained a Spanish colony, and the flag of Spain waved above the Zócalo. Then, in 1810, the Mexican people rose up against Spanish rule. They won their independence in 1821. The new nation suffered hard times and civil wars for the next hundred years. The worst civil war was fought from 1910 to 1920. More than a million Mexicans were killed.

Through the centuries of war and peace, the ruins of Tenochtitlán lay like silent ghosts under the streets of Mexico City. Now and then, tokens of the old civilization resurfaced to remind Mexicans of their ancient glory.

Cortés's men wrecked the great Aztec pyramids and built churches on the sites.

This Diego Rivera painting shows arms being distributed during a civil war in Mexico that lasted from 1910 to 1920.

Archaeologists working in Mexico City still find Aztec vases, figurines, seashells, and other items from the time of the Aztecs.

In 1790, workers digging a basement in the Zócalo area stumbled on a huge rounded stone. It proved to be the great Aztec Calendar Stone, a 26-ton disk covered with carvings that tell the story of Aztec history. The Calendar Stone is now displayed in Mexico City's famous National Museum of Anthropology. In the 1970s, a crew digging a trench for an electrical cable accidentally uncovered a great pyramid complex. Archaeological experts rushed to the scene, and over the next few years the area was carefully excavated. It is now preserved as an outdoor museum called *Templo Mayor* (Main Temple). The museum, next to the National Cathedral, stands today as a proud symbol of that long-ago era when Tenochtitlán was one of the world's greatest cities.

This great Aztec Calendar Stone was uncovered in 1790.

How big is Mexico City? Homero Aridjis, a Mexican environmentalist and poet, said, "This is not a city, it is a country." And it is big enough to be a country. There are more people in Mexico City than the total population of Guatemala, El Salvador, Honduras, and Nicaragua. Those countries of Central America are neighbors of Mexico. About 25 percent of all Mexicans live in the Mexico City region — on less than 1 percent of the country's land.

COME ONE, COME ALL

It's hard to take an accurate census in Mexico City because newcomers arrive from the countryside at the rate of 1,700 per day. In the mid-1990s, the city's population stood at almost 16 million. When the near suburbs are added, the figure zooms to about 22 million. Mexico City is the most populous urban center in the Western Hemisphere.

Such runaway growth is fairly new. In 1930, the city held 1 million people. By 1970, that number had jumped to 8 million. By 1980, it zoomed to 15 million. The population explosion began when farm machinery replaced manual workers in the country's rural areas. With fewer ways to make a living on the land, farm families had to move to the cities. All Mexican cities mushroomed in the 1970s and 1980s.

This flower vendor sells her wares from a canal boat in Xochimilco.

The capital, especially, grew at a startling rate. New people arrived in such great numbers that each year the population of Mexico City grew by about the size of San Francisco or Baltimore.

Many newcomers were "squatters." They set up shacks illegally in open fields on the outskirts of the city. Mexico City residents called the illegal settlers *paracaidistas*

paracaidista (PAH-RAH-KYE-DEE-STAH)

parachutists), because they came so quickly it seemed as if they simply fell from the sky. The squatter communities were known as *ciudades perdidas* (lost cities). No one knows how many lost cities there are in the capital. In the 1990s, a high wall was put up at the north end of the city to stop the spread of settlements. The city wanted to keep what little greenery was left in the Valley of Mexico.

The grandest of all the lost cities is a sprawling suburb with the tongue-twisting Aztec name Nezahualcoyotl. Residents simply call it Neza. In the late 1950s, Neza was a barren land of rocks and cactuses. Today, it has a population of almost 3 million. It is the country's third largest city. Though its residents are poor, Neza is something of a success story. In the beginning, the suburb was a collection of shacks with makeshift streets filled with rats and garbage. But Mexicans are very good at making the best of what little they have. The people of Neza bought a fleet of garbage trucks and gradually tore down their old huts. They replaced the huts with small brick houses. Neza is now a stable community with shops, schools, and hospitals. It stands as a dramatic example of a lost city that found itself.

Many residents of the "lost cities" look for useful items in the city dumps near their neighborhoods.

ciudades perdidas
(SEE-OOH-DAH-DEHS
PER-DEE-DAHS)

Nezahualcoyotl
(NET-SAH-WAHL-
COY-OHTEL)

This little girl is doing her best to clean up the space where she lives near a huge Mexico City dump.

It is the promise of jobs that brings farm people to the city. About one-third of the country's factories are in the capital. Mexico City is also the largest center for government employment. However, there are never enough jobs to fill the needs of the masses who arrive every day. More than 30 percent of the city's workforce is either unemployed or underemployed. Still, throngs of farm folk stream into the capital's bus stations. Even though the farm people trade the problems of rural poverty for those of urban poverty, Mexico City still shines to them as a beacon of hope.

POLLUTION—THE PRICE OF GROWTH

For more than 600 years, the people of Mexico City could see two magnificent mountain peaks on the southeastern skyline. The Aztecs, Spaniards, and Mexicans alike enjoyed that view. The mountains are ancient volcanoes whose tops are snowcapped even in midsummer. Their names are Popocatepetl and Ixtacihuatl. A folktale says they are husband and wife, and that when they quarrel thunder shakes the city. Today, young residents know of these mountains only from stories told by their grandparents. The Mexico City atmosphere is filled with haze from cars and factories. This smog acts as a shade that cuts off city dwellers from the marvelous mountain view.

The capital is home to 30,000 factories and 3.5 million cars, trucks, and buses. This combination pumps 11,000 tons of gaseous wastes into the air each day. Because the city rests in a bowl-shaped mountain valley, the waste material cannot escape. It becomes a brown fog that settles over the streets for weeks at a time. Drivers often need to turn their lights on even at high noon. Because of the pollution, about 2 million city dwellers suffer from chronic asthma.

Popocatepetl (POH-POH-KAH-TAY-PETEL)
Ixtacihuatl (ISH-TAH-SEE-WATEL)

These twin volcanoes—called Popocatepetl and Ixtacihuatl—can no longer be seen from Mexico City because the terrible smog cuts off the view (inset).

Even though nearly 5 million people use the Metro every day (below), midday traffic jams like this one (left) are common in Mexico City.

A huge number of people have eye irritations and shortness of breath. Lead from car emissions is especially harmful to children. The Mexican Ecology Movement claims that as many as 1 million city children have dangerous levels of lead in their blood. This condition can cause brain damage.

Cars cause the biggest pollution problem, yet every year more cars appear on the streets. The Metro (the subway system) does help to keep cars off the streets. Opened in 1969, the Metro now moves almost 5 million people daily. Stations are kept spotless, and rubber-tired trains speed people quietly from stop to stop. The fare is less than a nickel, so the Metro is the world's cheapest subway to ride. The subway trains are very crowded, however, especially during rush hours.

SHAKY GROUNDS

When the sun rose over Mexico City on September 19, 1985, its rays pierced the ever-present haze. It seemed like a normal morning. Then, at 7:18, the ground lurched violently. Tall buildings swayed. A deadly hail of plaster and window glass rained down on the sidewalks. Inside the apartment houses, floors gave way and collapsed one on top of another. One survivor who lived in a high-rise said, "I felt as if I were in an elevator going down."

It was the Day of the Quake, a morning no resident will ever forget. At least 9,000 people died, 30,000 were injured, and 95,000 were left homeless. Ten years later, many of the tall buildings damaged by the earthquake still stood empty. They were unsafe to live in and owners didn't have enough money to repair them. Also, no one wanted to spend money on the buildings when another great tremor could strike the city at any time.

This huge apartment building was demolished by wreckers after the earthquake of September 19, 1985.

Two months after the huge earthquake of 1985, these buildings had not been torn down.

Throughout its history, Mexico City has been shaken by deadly earthquakes. The National Cathedral has been rattled so often over the centuries that it is now braced up by steel scaffolding. This prevents its inner walls from tumbling down. Mexico City's position on an ancient lake bed makes it tremble even when a quake strikes far away. The great 1985 earthquake began in the Pacific Ocean, about 220 miles to the west. But its destructive forces fanned out over the one-time lake bed to shake the huge city. Some scientists say Mexico City is five times more quake-prone than are the California cities of San Francisco and Los Angeles.

A HUNGER TO LEARN

Walk the sidewalks of the capital any weekday morning and you'll see groups of children giggling as they scamper to school. Rules require them to wear uniforms. If you look closely, you'll notice that the uniforms are clean and pressed. In Mexican families, the children—not the parents—are expected to take care of their uniforms. The uniforms have to look proper because personal cleanliness is a grade that appears on a student's report card.

Students in their classroom on the first day of school at Luis Monzon Primary Sch

Almost half the capital's 22 million people are under the age of eighteen. Every year, more than a million young men and women leave high school and look for work in the city's tight job market. Those without an education face a lifetime of marginal employment and poverty.

Public schools in the capital are overcrowded. The average class has only one teacher for forty-five students. Children double up at desks, and three or four share a single textbook. Despite the crowded conditions, classrooms are orderly and work proceeds in a serious manner. Students who misbehave are expelled. All students are expected to complete homework assignments. Studying at home is very hard for those children who share a one-room dwelling with six or more family members. Still, most students manage to hand in their homework on time in the morning.

La República (LAH REH-POOH-BLEE-KAH)
chilango (CHEE-LAHN-GOH)

These Mexican children are enjoying their time away from school.

What's in a Word?

In conversation, Mexican people usually say *La República* (The Republic) when referring to their country, and *Mexico* when talking about their capital city. This is especially true in Mexico City, where a spoken reference to "Mexico" nearly always means the city, not the country. In slang, a Mexico City dweller is called a *chilango*. This word appeared in the 1980s and is now used all the time. No one knows its origin, nor can anyone translate *chilango* into English or any other language. If said in anger, it can be an insulting word, but in normal use "*chilango*" simply describes a fun-loving person from "Mexico."

School parades celebrating holidays are exciting events in the capital. During such parades, streets are closed to car traffic. The students march while the entire neighborhood watches. The school's drum and bugle corps usually leads the procession. As they march, a glow of joy lights up the students' faces. Such parades allow children to show their community they are proud—proud of their school, proud of their city, and proud to be Mexican.

The students below are marching in the Mexican Independence Day Parade.

These students are dressed for the flag ceremony held on the first day of school.

bazaar sábado (BAH-SAHR SAH-BAH-DOH)

Schoolchildren carry banners honoring 1910 hero Pancho Villa during a November 20 Revolution Day Parade.

San Angel

For centuries, San Angel was a town that lay south of Mexico City. Artists and writers lived there. In the 1920s, the famous artist Diego Rivera owned a home in San Angel. Beginning in the 1950s, San Angel was engulfed by Mexico City's growth. Houses and buildings from the ever-expanding capital spread out over the country-side and surrounded old San Angel. Today, San Angel is a neighborhood within the city. Other one-time suburbs of the capital are also just spots on a giant urban map.

Still, San Angel has kept much of its small-town charm. Its cobblestone streets are quiet amid the clamor of the big city. It has a central plaza that hosts an exciting event called *bazaar sábado* (Saturday special market). Jewelry, pottery, leather goods, and other handicrafts are displayed during bazaar sábado. Some of the items are cheap souvenirs, but others are beautifully made. San Angel is still known as a refuge for the country's best artists. Its residents proudly call San Angel "our town."

Mexico City is not only the country's capital and industrial hub, it is also its cultural center. Mexico's major art galleries, museums, theaters, book-publishing firms, and television stations are located there. A wide variety of sports are played in Mexico City; world-class restaurants operate there; and the country's best-loved parks serve the people on their precious days off.

A LOVE OF COLOR AND EXPRESSION

A strange change takes place in the Mexican men and women who enter an art museum. Even the poorest and the least educated behave as if they had just stepped into a church. Silently they study the paintings, noting the brushwork and the artists' use of color. Art—especially as it is expressed in murals—is a passion in Mexico City.

This colorful 1926 painting by Diego Rivera is called Flower Seller.

A portrait painter draws a crowd in Chapultepec Park.

Visitors to Mexico City's National Palace are drawn to the murals by Diego Rivera. The wall paintings show Rivera's view of Mexican history from its earliest days.

A mural is a painting on a wall or a ceiling. Some murals are painted on wet plaster. The paints sink in and the colors remain bright for years. The Aztecs painted murals on their temple walls. The Spanish painted murals on the walls and ceilings of their churches. After the Mexican Revolution of 1910-1920, there was a renewed interest in wall paintings. During this period, Mexican muralists became recognized as the greatest in all the world. The center of their artistic activity was Mexico City.

The Border *is a painting by Mexico City artist Frida Kahlo.*

Diego Rivera was the most famous of the post-Revolution muralists. Rivera once said that as a child he was driven to paint "just as a tree [is driven] to produce fruit and flowers." By the time he was three, Rivera had drawn so many pictures on the walls of his house that his father ran out to buy him a blackboard and plenty of chalk. Starting in 1929, Rivera painted his view of Mexican history on the inside walls of the National Palace at the Zócalo. He showed the Aztecs as peaceful farmers and the Spaniards as brutal invaders. He also showed a happy and prosperous new nation under a Socialist government. At the time, the flames of the Mexican Revolution still burned fresh in the people's hearts. Fistfights broke out between those who didn't like Rivera's Socialist politics and the art students who defended their master's freedom to paint what he chose. Such is the passion for art in Mexico City.

A 1940 photograph of artist Diego Rivera and his wife, artist Frida Kahlo

Artist Rufino Tamayo standing beside one of his paintings

Rufino Tamayo was born in 1899. He grew up with his aunt, who owned a fruit stand in the capital. As a toddler, Tamayo spent time in the city's open-air markets. He drank in the rich colors of limes, oranges, papayas, bananas, and other fruits displayed in the market stalls. In 1929, Tamayo completed his first true masterpiece, *Chair with Fruit*. It is a reflection of his childhood in the marketplace. Tamayo preferred to work on canvases rather than create wall paintings. Today, some of his best paintings are displayed at the Rufino Tamayo Museum near Reforma Boulevard in Mexico City. The museum was a gift from Tamayo and his wife to the men and women of the city. When the famous painter died in 1991, Mexico City factory workers, waitresses, and taxi drivers were seen weeping in the streets. Mexico City is one of the few cities in which a great painter is treated as a great man or woman.

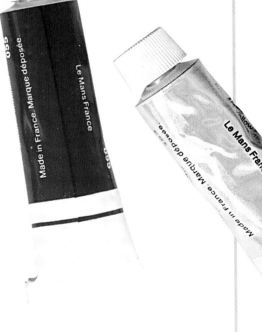

This painting, called Sandiás *(Watermelons), shows artist Rufino Tamayo's love of the rich colors of Mexico City's open-air markets.*

DEATH IN THE AFTERNOON

Carlos Arruza, Rodolfo Gaona, Silverio Perez, Lorenzo Garza, Manolo Espinosa. All these men are as popular as movie stars and are richer than corporation owners. Pictures of them hang in Mexico City's barbershops, billiard halls, *cantinas* (taverns), and other places where men gather. They gained their fame in the sands of the *plazas de toros*, the bullrings of the world. The largest such bullring is the stadium in Mexico City that seats 50,000 people. The heroes are bullfighters—*matadores*—dashing symbols of courage and manhood.

The bullfight, *corrida de toros*, is a Spanish import. In the years when Spain held sway over Mexico, bullfights were staged at the Zócalo. Today, bullfighting's greatest *aficionados* (fans) are found in Mexico and in Spain. The world's best *matadores* come to Mexico City to perform before cheering audiences.

*Bullfighters—*matadores—*are treated as heroes in Mexico.*

plaza de toros (PLAH-SAH DEH
  TOH-ROHS)
matador (MAH-TAH-DOHR)
corrida de toros (KOR-REE-
  DAH DEH TOH-ROHS)
aficionado (AH-FEE-SEE-OH-
  NAH-DOH)

Of course, other sports e closely followed in the exican capital. Soccer has ercely enthusiastic fans. apital residents also watch aseball, basketball, boxing, restling, tennis, and a ghtning-fast version of cquetball called *jai alai*. In 994, two National Football eague (NFL) teams, the *aqueros* (Cowboys) of allas and the *Petroleros* Oilers) of Houston, played an exhibition game in Mexico City. The game drew 120,000 fans, an NFL record.

But it is bullfighting that most affects the Mexican spirit, especially among males. The corrida recalls an era of knighthood when courage was the most important measure of a man. A matador stands alone in a ring facing a 1,000-pound animal that could kill him with a thrust of its powerful head. This is a fight to the death—but it is accompanied by music, flowers, and matadors in striking costumes. American writer Ernest Hemingway described the drama of bull-fighting in his book *Death in the Afternoon*.

Though it is loved by many, the corrida also has outspoken critics within and outside Mexico City. Defenders of the corrida say that these are special bulls, bred to fight. Critics insist the bull is a poor animal who is tortured in the ring and then, finally, is killed. The corrida poses an eternal question for which there is no easy answer: Is it high drama, or is it barbaric cruelty to animals?

jai alai (HIGH-LYE)

Mexican soccer players (in green shirts) played Bulgaria in this 1994 World Cup game.

ISLANDS IN THE METROPOLIS

The Monumento a los Niños Héroes *(Monument to the Young Heroes) stands at the entrance to Chapultepec Park.*

Parks and squares are islands of peace in the Mexican capital. Residents use them to escape from the busy pace of the modern city. Mexico City has so many such islands that even veteran taxi drivers don't know the names of all of them. But the famous parks and squares have been known and loved by generations of Mexico City's people.

These Mexican men have been riding their horses in Chapultepec Park.

Many Mexico City families enjoy weekend boating on one of Chapultepec Park's man-made lakes.

Chapultepec (CHAH-PUHL-TEH-PECK)

The National Museum of Anthropology in Chapultepec Park (below) displays artwork created by the ancient peoples of Mexico.

The grandest of all the city's parks is sprawling Chapultepec. It is a 1,000-acre reserve of greenery that becomes a carnival of life on the weekends. Fully 1 million people gather there each Sunday. The park has a zoo, a miniature railway for children, three boating lakes, two roller-skating rinks, a botanical garden, a polo field, and leafy glens that are perfect for family picnics. *Chapultepec* is an Aztec word. It means "Grasshopper Hill." Aztec emperors had summer houses and private hunting grounds there. A popular Chapultepec attraction today is a castle, parts of which date to 1783. The castle is now the National History Museum. It houses exhibits ranging from the conquest to the revolution. Also in the park is the National Museum of Anthropology. Truly one of the great museums of the world, it displays a wonderful collection of artwork created by the Aztecs and other ancient peoples of Mexico.

History comes alive at the *Plaza de Tres Culturas* (Plaza of Three Cultures). Every day, groups of schoolchildren in uniform are led there by their teachers. Schools teach Mexican history in three periods: the pre-Columbian period, the 300-year period of Spanish rule, and the modern era since the 1810–1821 War of Independence. In the Plaza of Three Cultures stand buildings that represent all three epochs: an Aztec pyramid, a sixteenth-century Spanish church, and a modern concrete-and-glass housing complex. Nowhere else in the nation do the three eras come together so neatly.

In the Plaza of Three Cultures (above) stand an Aztec pyramid, a Spanish church, and a modern housing complex.

This girl in Alameda Park had her face painted for the Day of the Three Kings (La Epifanía).

Plaza de Tres Culturas (PLA-SAH DEH TREHS KOOL-TOO-RAHS)
La Epifanía (LAH EH-PEE-FAH-NEE-AH)

52

Left: People enjoy relaxing at one of the beautiful fountains in Alameda Park.

Right: This statue of former Mexican president Benito Juárez is one of many statues in the park.

Alameda Park is an oasis of grass and trees in the heart of downtown. It is surrounded by tall buildings. The park is graced with elegant fountains and statues, but it has a fearful past. Spanish authorities once used the grounds to burn to death people accused of religious crimes. On the east end of Alameda Park stands the *Palacio de Bellas Artes,* the Palace of Fine Arts. It is a huge auditorium building where the world-famous ballet company, the Ballet Folklorico, performs.

Palacio de Bellas Artes (PAH-LAH-SEE-OH DEH BEH-YAHS AHR-TEHS)

These Ballet Folklorico dancers perform at the Palacio de Bellas Artes, a wonderful theater in Alameda Park.

Pedestrians walk past the Palacio Nacional (National Palace) on the edge of the Zócalo.

Certainly the most historic of all the plazas is the Zócalo in the city's center. Every morning at sunrise, a company of the nation's smartest-looking soldiers marches onto the Zócalo to raise the Mexican flag. In the center of the green, white, and red banner is the Coat of Arms of Mexico—a picture of an eagle sitting on a cactus with a

Palacio Nacional (PAH-LAH-SEE-OH NAH-SEE-OH-NAHL)

nake dangling from its
beak. It was here, on the
Zócalo grounds almost 700
years ago, that the Aztecs
claimed to have seen this
mystical eagle and immedi-
tely began to build a city.
The great city now spreads
in every direction—far
beyond the dreams of its
Aztec founders. And now,
every evening at dusk, the
soldiers march out a second
time to lower the green,
white, and red flag of
Mexico. All those who
watch the ceremony know
the flag will flutter again
when dawn breaks over
this, the oldest city in
the Americas and the
largest city in the Western
Hemisphere.

*Opposite: The National
Palace forms an impressive
backdrop for the daily flag-
lowering ceremony in the
Zócalo.*

The Palacio de Bellas Artes,
a Sinking Landmark

The *Palacio de Bellas Artes* building was erected at great expense between 1904 and 1934. The Mexican Revolution of 1910-1920 delayed the building's completion. Built of Italian marble, it was origi- nally intended to be the finest opera house on the American continent. Today, it is a spectacular building, but it also serves as a painful reminder that Mexico City rests on the muddy bed of an ancient lake. The building is simply too heavy for the ground underneath it. Since its construction, it has sunk lopsidedly nine feet into the soil below. Engineers will soon have to take on the huge problem of trying to keep this immense building afloat.

FAMOUS LANDMARKS

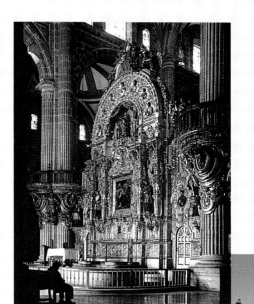

The Monument to Independence (left), is called El Angel, *the Angel, because of the statue on top of the column (right).*

The main altar of the National Cathedral

The National Palace

The Zócalo
Officially called Constitution Plaza, this large central square is in the heart of Mexico City; it was a public gathering place even in Aztec times.

The National Cathedral
Situated on the north side of the Zócalo, it is Mexico's most important church.

Templo Mayor
Near the National Cathedral, it contains the ruins of an Aztec pyramid complex that was uncovered in the 1970s.

The National Palace
A government building on the east side of the Zócalo, it boasts a brilliant set of murals painted by Diego Rivera.

The Museum of Mexico City
A five-minute walk from the Zócalo, this little-known museum contains fascinating exhibits from the Aztec era, the Spanish period, and the postindependence period.

The Metro
The capital's very efficient subway system moves 5 million people a day safely and without adding to air pollution.

Alameda Park
A wonderful place to relax or stroll in the heart of downtown.

Latin American Tower
At 44 stories, it is one of Latin America's tallest buildings; because it "floats" on special supports, it survived the major earthquakes that rattled the city in 1957 and again in 1985.

A lazy Sunday afternoon in Chapultepec Park

The Basilica of Our Lady of Guadalupe

The Latin American Tower

The Thieves' Market

Near downtown, this open-air market used to be a whispered-about spot that specialized in selling stolen goods; it is now a colorful market devoted to handmade crafts and artwork.

Reforma and Insurgentes Boulevards

The capital city's two major boulevards are always clogged with traffic. They were designed to look like the grand boulevards of Europe and still have some of their old elegance.

The Plaza of Three Cultures

The three eras of Mexican history are present here in an Aztec pyramid, a Spanish church, and a modern housing complex.

Chapultepec Park

One thousand acres of grass, trees, and lakes, the park is the favorite getaway place for Mexico City residents of all social classes.

The Museum of Anthropology

Situated in Chapultepec Park, this famous museum houses artifacts of all ancient Mexican cultures.

University City

Home of the National Autonomous University of Mexico (UNAM); founded in 1553, it now has some 300,000 students, making it the largest school in the Americas.

The Basilica of Our Lady of Guadalupe

About seven miles north of the city, it is here, legends say, that the Mexican patron saint Our Lady of Guadalupe appeared to a humble Indian man shortly after the Spanish Conquest.

FAST FACTS

AREA Mexico City: 579 sq. miles
Metropolitan Area: 883 sq. miles

ALTITUDE 7,575 ft. above sea level

CLIMATE Mostly warm and sunny during daylight hours, except in the rainy season from June through September. The average January temperature is 55 degrees Fahrenheit. The average July temperature is 63 degrees Fahrenheit.

INDUSTRIES Mexico City has about 30 percent of all the country's factories and almost 40 percent of its manufacturing jobs. Important products include automobiles, cement, drugs, furniture, iron and steel, and textiles. Printing is a major industry; the capital publishes about 20 different daily newspapers and many magazines. Mexico City is the headquarters of 30 radio stations and 5 major TV stations. The city's huge Benito Juárez Airport is one of Latin America's busiest. Tourism is an important element in the city's economy; about 17,000 hotel rooms and many restaurants are geared to the tourist trade.

CHRONOLOGY

1000 B.C.
Agricultural villages, whose people cultivate corn, develop in the Valley of Mexico

A.D. 1175
The Aztecs, a rootless people from the north, enter the Valley; they are impressed by the stone cities built by the older cultures

1325
At the southern end of the Valley, the Aztecs report seeing an eagle sitting on a cactus with a snake in its beak; this, they

believe, is a signal from a god commanding them to build a city

1510
The Aztec city, Tenochtitlán, holds almost 300,000 people and serves as the capital of the powerful Aztec nation

1519
A group of 600 Spanish adventurers, commanded by Hernán Cortés, land on Mexico's eastern shores at the present-day city of Veracruz

1521
After a long and bloody battle, the Spaniards defeat the Aztecs; the marvelous city of Tenochtitlán is wrecked during the fighting; Cortés immediately begins building a new metropolis—called Mexico City—on the site

1553
Spanish authorities found the University of Mexico in Mexico City, the first university in the Americas

1810
Father Miguel Hidalgo y Castilla gathers a peasant army in the state of Guanajuato and the Mexican War of Independence breaks out

1821
Independence leaders seize power in Mexico City, ending 300 years of Spanish rule

1836
U.S. settlers living in Mexico's northern province of Texas declare their independence

A weaver sells her colorful ponchos at the Xochimilco market.

1846
War erupts between the United States and Mexico

1847
A U.S. army commanded by General Winfield Scott occupies Mexico City

1848
Mexico cedes much of its northern territory, including present-day California and the southwestern states, to the United States

1876
A dictatorial army leader, Porfirio Díaz, becomes president and holds power in Mexico City for most of the next thirty years

1910
A revolution begins; its leaders, including Francisco Madero, Pancho Villa, and Emiliano Zapata, initially work to overthrow Porfirio Díaz

1920
The revolution, which killed more than 1 million Mexicans, slows to a halt

1964
The National Museum of Anthropology opens in Chapultepec Park

1968
Mexico City hosts the Olympic Games, making Mexico the first Latin American country to be so honored

1980
The population of Mexico City is 15 million, almost double that of 1970

1985
A terrible earthquake strikes the capital, killing at least 9,000 people

1990
The Mexico City region's population reaches almost 22 million, making it possibly the largest urban center in the world

MEXICO CITY

A	B	C	D	E	F	G	H	I	J	K

Map labels:
- Thieves' Market
- Plaza Garibaldi
- Reforma Boulevard
- Alameda Park
- Palace of Fine Arts
- National Cathedral
- Templo Mayor
- Benito Juárez statue
- Latin American Tower
- Zácalo Constitution Plaza
- National Palace
- Museum of Mexico City
- Monument to Independence
- National Museum of Anthropology
- Rufino Tamayo Museum
- National History Museum
- Monument to the Young Heroes
- Insurgentes Boulevard
- Chapultepec Park

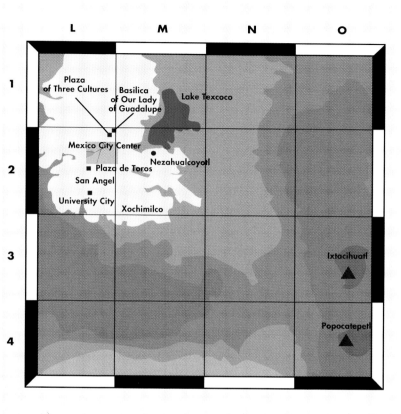

GLOSSARY

ancient: Very old

archaeological: Having to do with the study of ancient people

array: A large variety

census: An official count of people

chronic asthma: An ever-present, long-term, continuing lung disease that makes breathing difficult and causes coughing

culminating: Ending or leading to an end

environment: The condition of the natural surroundings, such as air, water, soil, plants, and animals

environmentalist: A person who is concerned with the environment

epoch: An era; a period of time in which important events take place

fosters: Encourages

human sacrifice: The ritualistic killing of people in order to meet the demands of the gods

marginal employment: A job that produces barely enough money to live on; underemployment

mime: A silent actor who entertains with gestures

misbehave: Act badly

nomads: Wandering people, those without an established home

pollution: Dirtying the environment with man-made wastes

poverty: The condition of being poor

refuge: A safe, secure, or comfortable place

sacred: Holy

spectacle: An interesting and noteworthy sight

squatters: People who settle without legal permission on land that is not legally their own

Picture Identifications

Photo Credits

INDEX

ABOUT THE AUTHOR

R. Conrad Stein was born and grew up in Chicago. He attended the University of Illinois, where he earned a degree in history. He is the author of dozens of other books for young readers. Mexico is Mr. Stein's second home. He lived in the country for seven years. He speaks Spanish and holds an advanced degree from the University of Guanajuato. He was delighted when Children's Press asked him to write this book about Mexico City. Mr. Stein now lives in Chicago with his wife and their daughter Janna.